Dedicated

to

My Grandson

Elliot King

Welcome

To The

Smoke House

Tales from

the

Smoke House

The Children's Book

by

Franklin P Smith

Illustrated by

Sylavanna Latrice Redding

Table of Contents

Ralph, The Magical Bear

Stanley, The Hippo

Oscar, The Ostrich

Harrie, The Easter Rabbit

Molly, The Cow That Jump over the Moon

The Legend of the Yellow Pumpkin

The Magical Pebbles

Chance, The Bear

Author's Notes

The stories in this collection come from many collections. They were written to share some of the meaning of life that has come to me over the years. This is especially true of Ralph the Magical Bear and Harrie the Easter Rabbit.

As I look back over my life, I can see the teachings and the philosophies that Rev. B. G. Munro and Mr. Franklin Watt, an old missionary who could build a house with only five tools, both taught me as a youth. Some of these stories are ethical, and they all reflect principles from the Bible and taught by God and His Son, Jesus Christ.

In a way, I wish that I could communicate to everyone those magical words
Ling Chang uses. I leave it to those hearing or reading these their own magical words, principles, and the pearls of wisdom buried in their lives.

I hope that whoever reads or tells these stories will enjoy them, as well.

With respect,

Franklin P Smith

Ralph the Magical Bear
(As told to me by Ling Chang)

There once was a little bear cub. He was like any small bear cub, full of curiosity and very mischievous. That was especially true of this cub. He had wandered off from the den where his mother had placed him and his sister. A butterfly had entered the cave and startled this little bear. His sister didn't pay much attention to the butterfly, but the little bear wanted to touch it.

The small bear started to chase the butterfly. He chased it out into the forest and chased and chased until he fell down a steep cliff. After his fall, the cub looked around and wondered how far he had roamed from home. He knew that he was lost.

The next thing to enter his mind was his growling stomach. He was hungry. He smelled some beautiful yellow flowers and ate them. This only made his stomach growl louder. He ran up the hill that he had fallen down. He thought that he could see his mother looking for him near the top. But he ran up the hill so quickly that he fell backwards down the hill again. This time he rolled into a large log.

When he sat up, he realized that he was in luck because he smelled the greatest delicacy, honey. His mother had found some for his sister and him only days before. But his luck did not hold out. While sniffing out the honey, the little cub got his head stuck in the hollow log, and the bees got the better part of the cub's nose. You should remember this part of the story.

I was walking to my house deep in the forest when I heard the thrashing of leaves off to my left. The noise grew more intense as I walked nearer this commotion. I stopped and started laughing at what I saw. There was this ball of fur with all four limbs thrashing in every direction. The bear's hind paws were digging two holes on each side of him. His front paws threw leaves in every direction while he was trying desperately to free his head from the hollow log.

Then I waved my hands and said the magic words to free him. Nothing happened. I said them again. Still nothing. I did this three times, but nothing would happen to the bear. I was surprised. I figured that the only reason my magic did not work was because the cub must have had some mighty power.

I started to walk toward the cub. I paused. I had seen over the years in the circus and carnivals

the results of bear attacks. When cornered, any sized
bear could have serious consequences for a human.

To ensure my safety, I waited until the cub was
totally exhausted. I gently stroked his furry back. I
did this several times before going further. Three
times I had to pull the cub's head out of the hollow
log. Each time, the poor cub yelped pitifully. I held
him with both of my hands on his midsection high in
the air. After I had freed him, the cub started to move
its hind legs erratically, trying to free himself from my
grasp. But I held the little furry animal tightly at arm's
length. Then I managed to maneuver the cub so that
I could see his face. His black nose was swollen four
times its normal size.

I was suddenly surprised when I realized that I
could communicate with this cub. He was saying,
"Let me down! Let me down! I want my mommy!"

I lowered him slowly to my level and looked
directly into his eyes. I saw the fierceness of this
bear, wanting his freedom. Yet underneath this, I saw
a great tenderness, greater than I ever known.

"I see underneath your meanness, little one.
You are sweet as the honey you were after," I said,
looking intensely into the cub's eyes. "You are like
Ralph Smith, whom I met at the Clown College. He
was the most ruthless man I thought I had ever
known, yet whenever I looked into his eyes, I saw the
gentlest spirit a human could have."

The little bear stopped struggling momentarily
and tilted his small black head to one side, but he said
nothing.

"Well, I am going to call you Ralph," I told him.
He blinked. "Now, Ralph, you have a choice when I
let you go. You can roam the forest and get your
head stuck in another log with no one to help you, or
you can become my friend and occasionally do tricks

for the people that I perform for," I said in a firm voice
and put him down on the ground in front of me. I
turned around and went on my merry way to my
house deep in the forest.

Ralph hesitated, but he did follow meat—at a
distance. I understood this. I am a human. No doubt
his mother had told him about humans killing and
being cruel to his kind.

It took several days for us to become friends.
The honey that I fed him did help.

Ralph soon grew to be eight and half feet tall.
Granted, he was small at first, but there is a reason
for this, and I will explain later how it came about.

Ralph and I travelled together, doing tricks for
the grown-ups and children who came to the carnivals
and the circuses we travelled with at that time. I
never gave our relationship a second thought until the
day the oldest elephant, Bo, went mad. Bo was forty-
years-old when he became raging mad.

I was pulling props from my large magical
chest when I was startled by Ralph's loud roar. After
his second roar, I looked up and saw him in front of
me. He was standing on his hind legs and roaring for
the third time. His face was vicious. He was ready to
attack whatever was behind me. I turned around and
saw Bo with both of front legs in the air. His trunk was
lifted upwards, and he was letting out a loud,
bellowing scream. I read Bo's mind. I could not
believe the anger and frustration he was feeling.

His legs fell to the ground and shook the earth I
was standing on. Bo must have weighed more than
15,000 pounds. At the same time, Ralph roared
again. I slowly raised my hands to calm Bo with the
magic I possess.

A shot rang out, and Bo fell to the ground. I
looked to my right where the shot had come from, and

there Don Juan, the carnival ring master, lowered his rifle, smoke twirling out of the long barrel. He was crying. He had been Bo's keeper since he was a youngster and had spent many hours with this animal.

I turned and Ralph was licking my left hand. He was sad that his friend Bo was no more. Ralph, I knew, did not understand about guns or death. Yet he knew that this would probably happen to him one day when he got old. I let Ralph sleep in my room that night.

Years went by as if they were days. Ralph grew and grew. Though he did not get taller, he gained weight from the honey I fed him four times a week. He did love that honey.

Several years after I had found him, I turned around one afternoon, and there was no Ralph. I stood silent for a minute, listening. I could hear Ralph's crying off in the distance. You are right. He had wandered off, looking for honey. He had smelled it in the wind.

I found him near the camp, stuck in a hollow log. I must admit that I laughed when I first saw him stuck in the log. I remembered the first time I met Ralph.

After I had pulled him out of the log, he tried to fight with the bees flying around him. The bees had bitten his nose again. It was swollen to four times its normal size—again. I changed my laughter to a soothing tone because I felt sorry for him. His love for honey was great.

Ralph grew to more than 800 pounds, but he still could jump through the fiery rings. I never thought of the magic he was showing me. I had to feed him the honey to keep him from wandering off to hunt it for himself.

We were doing a show with a small carnival in the Midwest years ago when it first happen. The crowd was nasty. There is no other way to describe the actions of the people. They were throwing cans and all sorts of trash at all of the performers.

When Ralph and I came into the arena, the crowd seemed to become more unruly. Ralph suddenly stood on his hind feet and let out an enormous roar. The crowd quieted a little. He roared three more times, and with each roar, the crowd became quieter and more subdued. They eventually hushed completely, waiting for us to perform.

Still up on his hind legs, Ralph surveyed the audience slowly. Then he looked at me, and four names appeared in my mind. I called them out. Four children came down and stood at the edge of the arena. They did not know what was going to happen. Frankly, I did not know what was going to happen. Ralph dropped to all four feet and walked slowly over to the first child, who climbed gleefully on Ralph's back. Ralph jumped through the ribbon-covered rings around the arena.

Ralph let the first three children ride in this manner while each child clamped on Ralph's huge back for dear life during the jumps. But after the circuit was completed, each child sat up, laughing loudly. After Ralph carried the three children, he rolled over on his back. Then the children all crawled up on his massive chest, giving the biggest hug possible for the large bear.

The last child to ride was a girl. She wore a blue denim dress and large-brimmed hat with two flowers on it—a pink and a red rose. She clamped and laughed the same as the other children did, but after sliding off his back, she walked around to face

Ralph. She took off her hat, arranged the roses on it, and placed it on Ralph's large head.

I stood amazed. The crowd remained silently. The small hat grew and grew until it fit Ralph's big bear head. (Remember, Ralph was a magical bear.)

By the next carnival stop, the word had spread about Ralph. Every child there had to come and hug him. After each of the children left, they all had expressions of sheer happiness.

You cannot imagine how the legend grew on the circuit about Ralph. He was the main attraction with the children, and my magic complemented what Ralph could do—not the other way around, as it once was. This new routine was fine with me, however, because we were a team. Also, it gave me more freedom to tell fortunes and develop magic tricks.

One night soon after, I heard Ralph growling a little in his sleep. I went into his room and watched his slight twitches while he dreamed. I stroked his short fur and felt his large body. I laid both hands on him.

I suddenly felt sad through what I found Ralph was thinking in his sleep: "I am so tried. My body hurts so much when the children jump on my back, but they make me feel so wonderful when they hug me. It is so hard to move my old bones in the morning. At night I hurt badly when I move."

I stroked his furry back all night. I remembered him as a cub, helpless in his hollow log. I recalled how he protected me from Bo, the mad bull elephant. I thought of all the children he had given joy to across our many years together.

I fed Ralph a large jar of honey that next morning. I did not have to say anything to him; he read my thoughts: "I know a way that you can always be held, hugged and cared about, and you can do the same for the people you want to be held and be hugged by. You will not be hungry any more nor will you feel any pain again."

Ralph raised his mighty body in the air and roared at the top of his voice. I said the magical words and waved my arms in the air four times. A large cloud of smoke materialized. After the cloud disappeared, there were eight teddy bears. Seven were each a foot tall, and one six inches tall. Each had a different hat on, and every hat had a tiny flower.

I shook at my amazement. I put the bears in my magical chest, ready for the next group of children.

Everyone needs something special every day.

Stanley the Hippo: The Hippo Who Loved the

Mud

Stanley, the hippopotamus, was born in the water just like other hippos. However, Stanley turned out differently from the other hippos.

He grew up nurtured by his mother, as most hippos do. And like the other hippos around him, he played King of the Hill, learning how to mark his own territory for when he became a fully grown male and would leave home. This is where he learned to love the mud.

Usually, when the young males played—if you would call it play—they charged at each other and pushed each other over on a muddy beach in Africa, where Stanley was born and lived. The mud stretched along the river where their parents stopped for the day and night.

Each day, Stanley went with his mother to learn how to find food and go into the water to wade or swim for most of the day.

Stanley liked to swim and to make noises underneath the water to the other hippos. This type of activity was what normal hippos are supposed to do because they could not stay out for long in the hot African sun. If a hippo were to stay out of the water all day, its tough, thick skin would dry and crack.

Yet Stanley was different.

His mother was the first to notice the habit he had taken up—rolling in the mud.

She always knew that Stanley would grow to be big and powerful, and she was right. He had entered the world weighing seventy-five pounds. Stanley's mother was very proud because most hippos weighed fifty pounds at birth. She knew he was unlike the other hippos, but she could not have guessed the love Stanley would have for mud.

She first found this out a few months after Stanley was born. After grazing for plants one morning, the pod returned to the river. She was under the water, but she felt that Stanley was not around. She surfaced, looked toward the shore, and saw Stanley playing with another hippo by bumping him into pools of mud. She watched Stanley roll back and forth in a pool of mud on the shore. Stanley's body was half-sunk into the pool.

Being a good mother, she galloped to Stanley's rescue, although he did not call it a rescue. Stanley was happy as he could be deep in that mud, even though he weighed nearly 200 pounds at the time.

His mother pushed him into the water, but Stanley went straight back to the pool of mud. His mother pushed him back into the water, telling him, "Hippos do not play in mud, Stanley! You will get stuck. Then the crocodiles will come and eat you, and the big birds will come to pick the meat off your bones. There will nothing left of you but your bones.”

Stanley frowned. He was unhappy in the river. He always had the time of his life when he was in the mud. The wet mud felt so good, especially when he was rolling in and out of it.

This routine happened every day after his mother and Stanley returned from finding food. However, he found the most marvelous way to play in the mud where his mother would not know what he was doing. He would practice fighting for territory with the other hippos on the river. Stanley would push the other hippos towards the mud pools, and then he let them push him into the mud. His mother, not realizing his plan, watched him play with the others and was so proud of him.

Stanley soon grew stronger and stronger— stronger than any adult hippopotamus. He gained weight until he reached more than 8,000 pounds and stood taller than six feet. His mother knew that her son would certainly have his choice of the females in the river to marry. She grew even more proud as Stanley’s strength and weight became known throughout the river region.

One day, though, a disaster happened. Stanley had gotten stuck in a deep mud pool. He could not get himself onto his feet. He weighed too much to raise himself up and out of the suction of the mud. He quickly realized he was stuck in the mud he loved so much.

The other male hippos were preparing to leave when his friend Buster asked Stanley if he needed some help.

“I sure would appreciate just a little,” replied Stanley. So Buster tried to push Stanley off his side, but he could not move Stanley much at all. He tried again and again, but the mud refused to let Stanley go.

"I cannot move you. You are just too big and weigh too much," Buster grunted. He left without another word. Stanley thought this would be the end of him.

"Surely, the crocodiles will come and eat me during the night," he murmured while he struggled to free himself. "The sun will dry my skin, and the big birds will peck until they pick my bones dry."

Stanley became more tired as time went by.

No one came for him.

The sun neared the horizon.

"It is only a matter of time before the crocodiles come," Stanley told himself. "My mother was right about playing in the mud. I should have done what she told me."

As the sun touched the distant treetops, Stanley had given up.

"Here we are!" Buster's voice rang out. "I had to find all of my friends. I knew just one hippo would not be enough, so I got everyone I could find!"

Stanley looked around at the six hippos. He was so happy to see them. Buster everyone along Stanley's big back. Very soon, all of the hippos were covered in mud, but after four attempts, he finally rolled out of the mud.

Stanley brushed up against each hippo to say thanks. Then he turned and ran splashing into the river. The water felt so good.

Stanley did not play in the mud for several days, but within a week, he was stuck again. Once more, his friends came to his aid and pushed him out of the mud. And once more, Stanley thanked them for their help before running into the river.

Watching these events was a young female hippo. Her name was Sheila. Stanley had already caught her eye.

The next time he was just about to get caught in the mud, Sheila was there, pushing him out and asking, "Do you not remember what happened last time?"

After Sheila had done this for the second time, Stanley knew that she must really like him. Stanley soon proclaimed her as his mate. No one protested his choice. What more could a hippo want in a mate other than someone to come to your aid so that you would not be eaten by the crocodiles?

As the years passed, Stanley did not notice how much Sheila watched over him. She let him play with other hippos where he could keep up his strength and weight. However, when he started to play around the mud pools, she would call Stanley to do some task or to teach Stanley Junior how to defend their territory. She knew that Stanley would show their son the joys of rolling in the mud, while also teaching him to beware of deep pools of mud, for the crocodiles and the birds would pick the meat from his bones.

Everyone needs help from another person.

Oscar the Ostrich
The Ostrich Who Didn't Like Himself

Oscar the Ostrich was born near the African shore of the Atlantic. Soon after he was born, his parents were killed by a wild boar. So Oscar was left by himself to pick the bare elements to find what he could eat to survive.

The days passed by quickly, and Oscar grew taller and bigger. Within three months, he weighed more than

100 pounds and had grown to over four feet tall. He was always hungry. He ate berries, and when he could catch a mouse, he would swallow it with only two gulps. Oscar was surprised how much he grew and, with each new day, how much faster he could run. He could even catch a rabbit if he wanted to.

As Oscar looked at the other animals all around him, he realized that he was very different from any other animal with feathers. For example, he noticed that he had only two toes instead of the four that the other birds had. So every day, Oscar looked for another bird like himself, but he could not find another to match him.

One day, he tried and tried to fly like the other feathered animals—those who seemed so similar to him. But at the end of the day, Oscar was exhausted and his wings ached from the constant flapping he had done. On the next day, he tried to jump off a tall rock, but his whole body fell straight down to the earth below. The fall bruised his two long legs.

Sometimes, while Oscar grazed, many of the other birds landed on his large, broad back. However, he started to run as soon as a bird perched on him. So the other birds would sit in a nearby tree and laugh at him. They had never seen anything like Oscar with his large head, big beak, and long, thick legs. His legs looked funny compared to their skinny, short ones. They made fun of Oscar's fluffy feathers whenever he flapped his wings. How awkward Oscar looked, reaching down to eat berries and running from the smaller birds. They would often ask Oscar when he was going to fly or if he just going to put his large head in a hole again as they had seen him do when was catching a mouse. Oscar started to feel that something was not right. He was sure that he was just a freak of nature. So whenever the birds would perch nearby and start to laugh again, he would find the nearest mouse hole or snake hole. Pretending to look for a meal, he would place his head inside where he could not hear the birds mock him.

As the months passed, Oscar finally became fully grown. He stood taller than six feet and weighed more than 400 pounds. His favorite food was still mice, but he could catch a snake with his two toes and crush its head by stepping on it with his other foot before the snake had the chance to bite him.

Once, Oscar encountered a pack of wild dogs. Although he was not bothering them, the dogs attacked, biting fiercely at his legs. Oscar quickly learned that his long, heavy legs could toss a dog a good distance—not to mention what a weapon his beak was. After the dogs were thrown aside, they never ventured to bother him again. Yet the dogs often joined the birds in laughing at him, so he kept hiding his head in the first hole that he could find. It was not always easy to find a hole he could fit his large head into so that he could not hear their laughter.

One day, while hiding from the birds' taunting, Oscar heard a voice out of the blue that was not laughing or making fun of him: "What are you hiding for?" Oscar ignored the voice as best he could, keeping his head firmly in the hole. Then a few minutes later, the voice asked again, "What are you hiding for?"

Oscar lifted his head slowly and saw a zebra, who said, "I've been watching you for several months, and I have to know. What are you hiding for?"

"They are picking on me again!" Oscar replied.

"Who is picking on you?"

"All the other animals."

"Oh, you're talking about those laughing hyenas and the birds," replied the zebra, walking towards him. Oscar walked a little closer, too, for he had never seen an animal with bold black and white stripes.

"Who are you?" Oscar asked.

"I'm Fred. I'm a horse."

"You're not a horse. Horses aren't white with black stripes—or black with white stripes for that matter," replied Oscar.

"I *am* a horse!" Fred insisted. "I'm of the horse family, just like you are of the bird family. You're acting just like those birds who make fun of you."

"I'm not like them at all," Oscar snapped. "I can't fly. My feathers are fluffy, not slick like theirs. I tried and tried to fly, but I couldn't. I'm not a bird! I'm too big to be a bird!" Oscar strode away.

"Wait! Wait! Wait! Hear me out!" Fred cried.

Oscar stopped and turned only his long neck and head around. "What?"

There was only the sound of birds' chirping in the nearby tree and the distant elephants' trumpeting. "Come back here, and I will tell you where there are other birds just like you," Fred said.

"There're others like me?! Where?" Oscar then turned his whole body so it was facing in the same direction his head.

"Yes, I've seen other birds like you. They're some as big as you and little ones, too," Fred replied.

"But where are they?"

"Listen," Fred said as Oscar moved directly in front of him. "Being the kind of animal I am, I have walked over long distances and seen many things."

"I don't believe you," Oscar snorted. "All you want to do is to make fun of me. You're just like everyone else."

"I'm telling you the truth. You are a bird—just like those perched in the trees over there. You have feathers, don't you?" Fred asked.

"Yes, but they are different from theirs."

"Do you agree that I am a horse?"

"Yes. No…" Oscar hesitated. "Either you're a horse or not a horse!"

"I'm a kind of horse," Fred replied. "I'm a part of the horse family in the same way that you're a part of the bird family. You simply can't fly. You can't fly because your fluffy feathers won't hold any air like theirs will."

Oscar seemed to accept Fred's theory, temporarily at least.

"Once," Fred continued, "a long, long time ago, there was a bird so big that it could have picked up an elephant."

"What happened to it?" Oscar asked.

"No one knows for certain," Fred replied. "It just disappeared. So I'm telling that you don't have to be ashamed of the way you look, or of who you are."

"Then where are the birds like me?" Oscar asked.

"Over those mountains," Fred nodded at the range in the distance. "The grasslands on the other side is where I last saw birds like you. It was several months ago, though."

"How did I get all the way over here?" Oscar asked.

"Your bird family still roams the plains in search of food. But when you were young, something must have happened to your parents, so you wandered."

"I have to go to find my kind," Oscar turned and started to walk toward the range.

"Wait! Wait! Wait!" Fred cried. "You don't know the way."

"Wait? Wait for what?" Oscar stopped, but again, he did not turn around. He aimed his body at the mountains and craned his neck to look at Fred.

"For me," Fred said, walking toward Oscar. "You'll get lost. You don't know where to go. I can show you the path I took to cross the mountains."

"But what do you want out this?" Oscar shifted his body around, still looking at the zebra.

"I'm going that way, too," Fred said, walking toward the mountains. "I'd simply like to travel with you." With that, the two turned towards the mountains.

The trip was long, and the mountains were far away. Fred and Oscar spent several weeks walking up to the mountain range and along the path that crosses it. They eventually descended towards the grassy expanse of the plains.

As soon as they reached level ground again, they spotted a herd of zebras under the shade of some trees.

Oscar stayed back as Fred went to greet the herd. Fred returned and told Oscar that the birds like him lived just over a nearby hill beyond the river. "About another day's travel," Fred reassured him. "And then you'll see others like you, your family."

Oscar toed at a clump of grass. He was both excited and scared.

Sensing his friend's feelings, Fred beamed. "You'll never have to hide your head in a hole again," he said.

Oscar walked quickly, for he was anxious to be with birds like himself. He crested the hill, and in the valley below, he could see dozens of other birds like himself. He watched each of the flocks for several minutes. The bigger birds were picking at the grasses or grooming themselves, while the little ones ran together in playful groups.

Easing himself slowly towards the nearest flock, Oscar realized that he had no idea what to say. So he simply told them about where he had grown up and about meeting Fred and their long journey to this place. The other birds listened intently with their heads tilting at various angles. When he talked about the abuse from the flying birds, he told them of his habit of sticking his head in a large hole so that he could not hear their teasing.

Some say this last part of the story was a mistake, that Oscar should not have told the other ostriches this part because to this day, it is rumored that ostriches will hide their heads in holes when they are scared or do not want to be bothered by their surroundings. However, no one has seen an ostrich actually hide like that.

Eventually, Oscar found a mate and had numerous offspring. He made it a point to tell them about his zebra friend Fred and the lesson Fred had taught him: Ostriches are a part of the bird family.

We are all part of a larger family, and we should treat other people likewise.

Harrie the Easter Rabbit

(As told to me by Ling Chang)

Once, years ago, I wedded the most beautiful woman ever known. However, that is another story, and I will tell more about that at a later time because there is no reason for you to know those things at present. For now, though, you should know that we had a cottage deep in the woods.

After the second or third year of marriage, we came home from Africa for the winter. I had just planted my flower garden for my beautiful Julie. She loved flowers so much. She would never let me pick them because they would die before their time. She was so sensitive and beautiful.

One morning in early May, I walked out into the flower garden and noticed that the tops of several flowers were gone. Curious, I returned the next day to inspect the flowers, and more tops were missing. I mentioned this to Julie. She told that spied a little rabbit jumping across the road when she was coming home the day before. I knew that this rabbit was eating the flower tops. So I made a trap from a box with a stick holding one end up. To the stick, I tied a carrot, which I placed carefully far under the box.

On the next morning, I discovered that this particular rabbit did not like carrots. I also found more of the flowers with their tops eaten off. Then, with surprise, I noticed that this little critter would skip certain flowers. In examining the flowers more closely, I found the rabbit only ate those that were at their peak of beauty. The others he left.

This was certainly not any ordinary rabbit.

I tried to catch the rabbit with the box again, using lettuce under it. Again, I had no luck.

Over the next two to three weeks, I tried all kinds of temptations under the box, but I failed to catch the thief. Then the rabbit stopped visiting our gardens.

Soon after, Julie and I went on tour late for the spring and summer. We then travelled to the Clown College in Tampa, where we stayed for the winter months.

In early spring, just before the last frost, we returned to our cottage in the woods. We tended the flower garden. Julie was so happy when the flowers came up quickly, and they all had a deep green color to their leaves.

One warm day, I was pulling weeds in the flower bed while Julie worked in the vegetable garden. As I stood up to stretch my back, a large rabbit jumped over my right foot.

"What nerve this rabbit has! This is our flower garden not his," I complained to Julie. I knew as good as my name was Ling Chang that this was the same rabbit who had eaten the tops of the flowers the previous year.

That night I sent a letter to the Greatest of Trappers, Harrie Turnipseed. (I must tell you more about him one day.) Several days later, he came with a spring-activated wire cage. Harrie assured me that this trap would capture the biggest and orneriest rabbit whoever jumped on the face of the earth. I told him that this rabbit was a different creature and explained how he was so selective in the flowers he would eat. However, Harrie reassured me that this trap could catch any varmint.

I picked several of the blooms for bait, although Julie was not happy about my doing so. I chose only those that I thought this varmint would like to eat. For four days, I placed the flowers in the trap, and for four days, there was no rabbit in the cage.

I was beginning to think that Harrie Turnipseed had finally met his match with this rabbit. Then I realized why I could not get this varmint to go into the cage and spring the trap.

At breakfast of the following day, I asked Julie if she would go and pick three blooming flowers. I had a theory of why and what would get the rabbit to eat the flowers. Julie did not want to catch the rabbit because she did not want to him to get hurt, even if it meant letting him eat all her flowers.

After she made me promise not to harm the little furry creature, she picked the flower petals for me, which she then arranged in the cage just as I had asked.

The next morning, I rushed out to the cage, and I saw that I had finally caught my little friend. He was a fat rabbit. He must have been eating every bloom for miles around. I squatted down to study the rabbit and cage carefully, and I knew my theory was correct. This rabbit was definitely different from any other I had ever heard of.

I picked up the cage. I could feel the fear in the furry creature. Our eyes met. Because of my powers, he understood when I said, "I will not hurt you. I promised my lovely wife that I would not harm any of your fuzzy fur."

I put the cage down, unlatched the door, and lifted him out. I could feel every muscle in his small body trembling.

"Please," he exclaimed in a high pitched voice. "Please do not feed me to the Big Bad Wolf or let the dogs get me. Your flowers are so sweet and special. Someone special must have been planting and caring for them very much."

"But you have eaten the petals off of most of my flowers. I should throw you to the dogs or ship you where you can do no more damage to my flower bed." I said sternly, looking deep into his big, black eyes. (I still remember his eyes clearly because they were always the same way from the first day we met. Ah, if he had only know what I saw in them!)

"I will make you an offer," I said. "You can live here with my wife and me, but you cannot eat our flowers. I will feed you will and keep you in a warm bed. I will use you in only one trick in my magic act. I will call you 'Harrie.'" I paused to give this creature time to decide what he wanted to do with my offer. He seemed reluctant, but I knew that one day the dogs would hunt him down.

"If you do not want accept my offer, I will give you to Harrie the Trapper. He will put you in a cage and feed you food—probably that you will not like," I said in a firm voice.

Harrie the rabbit agreed to my terms. I was so glad because Julie would have never have let me give him to Harrie Turnipseed.

I waited many months to use Harrie in my act because he and I needed to get used to each other. I wanted him to become accustomed to my ways and to be comfortable with me. I also wanted to reduce his enormous weight so that he could get into my black felt top hat.

Years went by, and Harrie brought get delight to many children in many places. Harrie and I were glad that he decided to live with Julie and me.

However, Harrie gradually gained his weight back. I suspected that Julie was sneaking extra food to him. By the end of the tour, I feared that he would grow too big for the act over the winter. Sure enough, Harrie gained more weight while we were in Tampa, and I was certain that he would never fit into my magical hat again. I would have to think of another act for him.

When spring came around again, I prepared my props for the first show of the season. I picked up my black top hat to dust it off. Making sure it was empty, I placed my hand inside. As I pulled my hand out, I was surprised that I held Harrie by the ears!

From then on, I pulled Harrie out of this hat, no matter what his size. After that, Harrie was different in other ways. I would pull him out of the hat, and then I would place him on the magical table next to the felt hat. At first, I did not mind him jumping down and climbing into the laps of the children around the stage. There were always giggles coming from the children as Harrie would rest for a moment in their laps.

One child that I remember was a little boy in a small wheelchair. Harrie was not in the boy's lap, but on his shoulder, whispering magical words into the boy's ear. The boy grinned.

Harrie would actually do this several times during performances and then hop back to the magical table. I usually did not pay much attention because of needing to concentrate on doing my magical tricks.

This version of our act went on for several years. Harrie was for great for act because he entertained the children while I catered to the adults in the audience. Every time I glanced at Harrie as he moved through the children sitting on the floor in front my magical table, I noticed that he would leave one child with a broad smile that seemed to come from the soul.

Then, one day, as I put Harrie in the black top hat, his ears were sticking out of the top.
A couple weeks later, I noticed that every time that I pulled Harrie out of the that, his ears would get a little longer.

The time soon came that I started to place Harrie upside down in the hat and pull him out by his legs. I know that might sound cruel, but the kids loved this. It was the only way Harrie would fit in the hat. I had no replacement off-stage waiting to take Harrie's place. All the while, Harrie did a great job of entertaining children while I did my acts for the adult crowd.

I still do not know how Harrie made it through the final show of the carnival tour because not only had his ears gotten longer, but so too had his legs. But make it he did. Then Julie, Harrie, and I went down to Tampa for the another winter at the Clown College. During this time, I noticed how awkward he was as he jumped around.

When the warmer days came, we went back to the cottage deep in the woods. Once again, I planted Julie's favorite flowers in the garden. At the end of each day, when the slight chill returned to the cottage, Harrie would jump clumsily on to Julie's lap, and she would stroke his furry body for hours.

I noticed that after the flower blooms came, none of them were being eaten. I knew what was happening. So I went to a nearby field and picked seven yellow daffodils. I knew that these were Harrie's favorites. I placed them in front of Harrie as he laid beside the fire. I blinked my eyes, and they were gone.

"Harrie, I understand what you need," I said, stroking his long ears. "Believe me, I know a farm where you will happy forever. You have given the children joy at every performance. You have given them the beautiful secret, and they will give that same secret to other for the rest of their lives."

I stood up, and Harrie rose on his hind legs. I said those magical words—the same ones Harrie had given to all those children. A great puff of white smoke appeared, and when it cleared, there was Harrie the Easter Rabbit. I then placed him in my magical trunk.

You know what is strange? He disappears from this trunk at the oddest times, especially during the spring. There is only one time I know that Harrie will not be there: Easter. You know that rabbit always

31

had a sweet tooth. So he still appears on doorsteps at Easter time.

Everyone needs to be told that they have special something.

Molly the Cow:
The Cow Who Jumped over the Moon

One summer, Charlie D. came to visit Jack's family farm to spend some time with them. Young Jack was about to begin school for the first time. Both of Jack's parents thought Charlie D.'s visit would be good for Jack because where they lived, he rarely saw or played with any other children.

Charlie D. was quickly nicknamed "CD" by Jack's parents. CD was three years older than Jack.

He was also twenty pounds heavier and nearly three heads taller.

During these warm months, CD and Jack took to each other quickly. Both woke up early, helped with the morning chores, and then ate their lunch. After lunch, they often disappeared until Jack's mother called them twice for supper.

Through table conversation, Jack's mother found out that Jack and CD usually went down to the small pond to play pirates or out to the big, red barn to play cowboys and Indians. After dinner, Jack's father would usually practice the fiddle while the boys helped Jack's mother clean up, tapping their toes to the music. Jack's parents thought things were going better than they expected.

However, this changed when CD and Jack spent a week with Jack's grandparents. At the end of the week, both boys appeared unannounced at the front door of Jack's house. With his head hanging low, Jack reluctantly gave his father a note from his grandfather, which read, "Watch out for this mischievous boy, and do not send him back to our house." Jack's father knew immediately this "boy" was not Jack, for he had spent many trouble-free nights with his grandparents.

Not saying a word, Jack's father studied both of the boys for several long moments. Their body language indicated trouble, but he knew not to ask for details in front of Jack's mother. Jack's father soon found out from his father that during the boys' stay, the house cat disappeared, they ate nearly all the food in the house, and they burned down the old feed shack. Jack's father decided not to ask CD for an explanation because CD was from the city, and he suspected that CD knew all the lies to get out of whatever city folk would be confronted with. Jack's father knew that many city slickers were just that way.

The next evening, Jack's father took his son to the side and asked him how he enjoyed their stay at his grandparents' house. Jack quickly confessed that CD had picked up the cat by its tail and swung it around and around, laughing as the cat tried to scurry away dizzily. Jack then told his father that CD raided the icebox at night and ate all the leftovers.

When Jack's father asked him about the feed shack, Jack said nothing as he picked at his fingernails. However, after his father promised not to spank him, he told him what had happened: "We were just playing, honestly, Poppa. CD found some candles and matches from the cupboard next to the stove. We took them out the old shack and lined up all the candles. Even though they were tall, I easily jumped over them, even when we lit them. But CD couldn't do it without knocking them over," Jack said with a little pride in his voice, but Jack's father face remained stern.

Jack continued, "And I got quicker each time, too. So CD started saying in a silly voice, 'Jack be nibble. Jack be quick. Jack jump over the candle stick.' I was having so much fun. CD tried hard, but he's so big, he couldn't jump high enough to clear the flames. When he knocked a candle down, we always blew it out," Jack paused. His father waited.

"But one set the straw on fire. We didn't have any water, and the fire spread quickly. So CD said that we'd better go down to the pond to get some water. When we came back, Grandfather was putting out the fire. He didn't look happy."

Jack's father almost sent CD home when he learned these details, but Jack's mother reminded him, "Boys will be boys." Knowing they had barely escaped serious trouble, CD and Jack played quietly near the house for a few days.

However, they soon fell back into their old routine, roaming the farm and playing just as they had done before.

On the last Saturday night of CD's stay, Jack's parents took the boys to a square dance at a local hall. Both CD and Jack loved the excitement. There were all kinds of food and colorful drinks. They were thrilled by the music and by seeing Jack's father play the fiddle with the band.

The next day, the boys spent the afternoon on the porch playing imaginary instruments. Then Jack asked for one of his mother's old wooden spoons. He loved the sound that he made hitting it against a solid piece of wood. CD found a branch and sang while he played his pretend guitar.

After three days of CD's singing, Jack said CD could scare the devil if he could hear him. CD kept on singing as he picked up another shorter stick, and as he pulled one stick along the other, he claimed he was the best fiddler in the world. Jack's mother soon told them that they would either have to get out of earshot or quit playing their instruments.

After lunch, both CD and Jack disappeared. Jack's mother was so pleased to have peace again that she did not ask them where they were going. While she enjoyed the quiet bustle of the farm, she did not notice that CD had slipped back into the house to grab Jack's father's fiddle.   Jack followed CD into the big, red barn, where Molly, the family's milk cow, hid from the afternoon sun in the corner of her stall, taking a nap. Although Jack did not really like how CD had teased Molly from the first day that he had arrived, Jack usually joined in, doing what most any boy would do to a cow: they took turns sneaking up behind her and then quickly running away after pulling her tail hard. Because of this, Molly watched for CD, and when she saw him nearing the barn, she quickly escaped to the shade of the woods nearby.

Smiling broadly, CD sat on a crate in the stall, placed the fiddle underneath his chin, and ran the bow across the strings. He pulled down and up steadily, making a strange, rhythmic screech. Jack started to pound in time on the side of the barn.

The house cat, May Bell, was stretched out near Molly's napping spot. Being very old, May Bell could barely hear the loud noise the two boys were making. From the reaction of her swinging tail, May Bell seemed pleased by what she could hear. They spent hours like this, happy to be making their so-called music.

On CD's last night on the farm, Jack's mother excused them after dinner to play one last time together. Daylight was fading, but they played under the big, bright harvest moon. While she cleaned up dinner, humming to herself, Jack's father reclined in his favorite chair and napped.

But quietly, CD snuck into the house and grabbed the fiddle and bow. Jack and CD ran out to the barn and jumped the gate to Molly's stall. They started to play their music again, softly at first, but they were soon screeching and banging loudly. Molly was trapped in the far corner of the stall, and unlike May Bell, she could hear well. As soon as the noise began, she got up and started to move around the stall, looking an opening. As the intensity and volume grew, Molly paced more quickly.

In the glow of the huge, yellow moon, Molly looked for a gap between the two boys. At that moment, CD pulled the bow hard along the strings of the fiddle, making the loudest high-pitch sound anyone has ever heard. With that, Molly suddenly bolted between them, jumped over the fence, and ran into the woods.

Jack came running around the corner of the barn in the bright moonlight, crying out, "Poppa, Molly just jumped over the moon!"

CD returned to the city early the following morning, but Jack and his father spent days trying to coax Molly out of the woods and back to her stall. After she was satisfied that CD was not hiding in the corner with a fiddle, she went back to her familiar corner. However, she would not let anyone even so much as touch her for several more days. It was another two weeks before Jack's father could get any milk from her.

That fall, when Jack went to kindergarten, he told everyone how his cow had jump over the moon. He told the same story to anyone who would listen. Over the years, this story changed by word of mouth into the saying, "The cow jumped over the moon." The only thing left out was the name of the cow: Molly.

Interestingly, long after CD's exploits were forgotten, Molly still bolted at any loud noise. In fact, she jumped the stall's fence nearly other month. Jack's father finally sold Molly to a traveling Medicine Man, who returned to the farm years later and told Jack, "Molly jumped a six-foot fence late one evening. We looked for weeks, but we could not find her."

There are always different ways at looking at events around us.

Molly the Cow: The Cow Who Jumped over the Moon

One summer, Charlie D. came to visit Jack's family farm to spend some time with them. Young Jack was about to begin school for the first time. Both of Jack's parents thought Charlie D.'s visit would be good for Jack because where they lived, he rarely saw or played with any other children.

Charlie D. was quickly nicknamed "CD" by Jack's parents. CD was three years older than Jack. He was also twenty pounds heavier and nearly three heads taller.

During these warm months, CD and Jack took to each other quickly. Both woke up early, helped with the morning chores, and then ate their lunch. After lunch, they often disappeared until Jack's mother called them twice for supper.

Through table conversation, Jack's mother found out that Jack and CD usually went down to the small pond to play pirates or out to the big, red barn to play cowboys and Indians. After dinner, Jack's father would usally practice the fiddle while the boys helped Jack's mother clean up, tapping their toes to the music. Jack's parents thought things were going better than they expected.

However, this changed when CD and Jack spent a week with Jack's grandparents. At the end of the week, both boys appeared unannounced at the front door of Jack's house. With his head hanging low, Jack reluctantly gave his father a note from his grandfather, which read, "Watch out for this mischievous boy, and do not send him back to our house." Jack's father knew immediately this "boy" was not Jack, for he had spent many trouble-free nights with his grandparents.

Not saying a word, Jack's father studied both of the boys for several long moments. Their body language indicated trouble, but he knew not to ask for details in front of Jack's mother. Jack's father soon found out from his father that during the boys' stay, the house cat disappeared, they ate nearly all the food in the house, and they burned down the old feed shack. Jack's father decided not to ask CD for an explanation because CD was from the city, and he suspected that CD knew all the lies to get out of whatever city folk would be confronted with. Jack's father knew that many city slickers were just that way.

The next evening, Jack's father took his son to the side and asked him how he enjoyed their stay at his grandparents' house. Jack quickly confessed that CD had picked up the cat by its tail and swung it around and around, laughing as the cat tried to scurry away dizzily. Jack then told his father that CD raided the icebox at night and ate all the leftovers.

When Jack's father asked him about the feed shack, Jack said nothing as he picked at his fingernails. However, after his father promised not to spank him, he told him what had happened: "We were just playing, honestly, Poppa. CD found some candles and matches from the cupboard next to the stove. We took them out the old shack and lined up all the candles. Even though they were tall, I easily jumped over them, even when we lit them. But CD couldn't do it without knocking them over," Jack said with a little pride in his voice, but Jack's father face remained stern.

Jack continued, "And I got quicker each time, too. So CD started saying in a silly voice, 'Jack be nibble. Jack be quick. Jack jump over the candle stick.' I was having so much fun. CD tried hard, but he's so big, he couldn't jump high enough to clear the flames. When he knocked a candle down, we always blew it out," Jack paused. His father waited.

"But one set the straw on fire. We didn't have any water, and the fire spread quickly. So CD said that we'd better go down to the pond to get some water. When we came back, Grandfather was putting out the fire. He didn't look happy."

Jack's father almost sent CD home when he learned these details, but Jack's mother reminded him, "Boys will be boys." Knowing they had barely escaped serious trouble, CD and Jack played quietly near the house for a few days.

However, they soon fell back into their old routine, roaming the farm and playing just as they had done before.

On the last Saturday night of CD's stay, Jack's parents took the boys to a square dance at a local hall. Both CD and Jack loved the excitement. There were all kinds of food and colorful drinks. They were thrilled by the music and by seeing Jack's father play the fiddle with the band.

The next day, the boys spent the afternoon on the porch playing imaginary instruments. Then Jack asked for one of his mother's old wooden spoons. He loved the sound that he made hitting it against a solid piece of wood. CD found a branch and sang while he played his pretend guitar.

After three days of CD's singing, Jack said CD could scare the devil if he could hear him. CD kept on singing as he picked up another shorter stick, and as he pulled one stick along the other, he claimed he was the best fiddler in the world. Jack's mother soon told them that they would either have to get out of earshot or quit playing their instruments.

After lunch, both CD and Jack disappeared. Jack's mother was so pleased to have peace again that she did not ask them where they were going. While she enjoyed the quiet bustle of the farm, she did not notice that CD had slipped back into the house to grab Jack's father's fiddle.   Jack followed CD into the big, red barn, where Molly, the family's milk cow, hid from the afternoon sun in the corner of her stall, taking a nap. Although Jack did not really like how CD had teased Molly from the first day that he had arrived, Jack usually joined in, doing what most any boy would do to a cow: they took turns sneaking up behind her and then quickly running away after pulling her tail hard. Because of this, Molly watched for CD, and when she saw him nearing the barn, she quickly escaped to the shade of the woods nearby.

Smiling broadly, CD sat on a crate in the stall, placed the fiddle underneath his chin, and ran the bow across the strings. He pulled down and up steadily, making a strange, rhythmic screech. Jack started to pound in time on the side of the barn.

The house cat, May Bell, was stretched out near Molly's napping spot. Being very old, May Bell could barely hear the loud noise the two boys were making. From the reaction of her swinging tail, May Bell seemed pleased by what she could hear. They spent hours like this, happy to be making their so-called music.

On CD's last night on the farm, Jack's mother excused them after dinner to play one last time together. Daylight was fading, but they played under the big, bright harvest moon. While she cleaned up dinner, humming to herself, Jack's father reclined in his favorite chair and napped.

But quietly, CD snuck into the house and grabbed the fiddle and bow. Jack and CD ran out to the barn and jumped the gate to Molly's stall. They started to play their music again, softly at first, but they were soon screeching and banging loudly. Molly was trapped in the far corner of the stall, and unlike May Bell, she could hear well. As soon as the noise began, she got up and started to move around the stall, looking an opening. As the intensity and volume grew, Molly paced more quickly.

In the glow of the huge, yellow moon, Molly looked for a gap between the two boys. At that moment, CD pulled the bow hard along the strings of the fiddle, making the loudest high-pitch sound anyone has ever heard. With that, Molly suddenly bolted between them, jumped over the fence, and ran into the woods.

Jack came running around the corner of the barn in the bright moonlight, crying out, "Poppa, Molly just jumped over the moon!"

CD returned to the city early the following morning, but Jack and his father spent days trying to coax Molly out of the woods and back to her stall. After she was satisfied that CD was not hiding in the corner with a fiddle, she went back to her familiar corner. However, she would not let anyone even so much as touch her for several more days. It was another two weeks before Jack's father could get any milk from her.

That fall, when Jack went to kindergarten, he told everyone how his cow had jump over the moon. He told the same story to anyone who would listen. Over the years, this story changed by word of mouth into the saying, "The cow jumped over the moon." The only thing left out was the name of the cow: Molly.

Interestingly, long after CD's exploits were forgotten, Molly still bolted at any loud noise. In fact, she jumped the stall's fence nearly other month. Jack's father finally sold Molly to a traveling Medicine Man, who returned to the farm years later and told Jack, "Molly jumped a six-foot fence late one evening. We looked for weeks, but we could not find her."

There are always different ways at looking at events around us.

Molly the Cow: The Cow Who Jumped over the Moon

One summer, Charlie D. came to visit Jack's family farm to spend some time with them. Young Jack was about to begin school for the first time. Both of Jack's parents thought Charlie D.'s visit would be good for Jack because where they lived, he rarely saw or played with any other children.

Charlie D. was quickly nicknamed "CD" by Jack's parents. CD was three years older than Jack. He was also twenty pounds heavier and nearly three heads taller.

During these warm months, CD and Jack took to each other quickly. Both woke up early, helped with the morning chores, and then ate their lunch. After lunch, they often disappeared until Jack's mother called them twice for supper.

Through table conversation, Jack's mother found out that Jack and CD usually went down to the small pond to play pirates or out to the big, red barn to play cowboys and Indians. After dinner, Jack's father would usually practice the fiddle while the boys helped Jack's mother clean up, tapping their toes to the music. Jack's parents thought things were going better than they expected.

However, this changed when CD and Jack spent a week with Jack's grandparents. At the end of the week, both boys appeared unannounced at the front door of Jack's house. With his head hanging low, Jack reluctantly gave his father a note from his grandfather, which read, "Watch out for this mischievous boy, and do not send him back to our house." Jack's father knew immediately this "boy" was not Jack, for he had spent many trouble-free nights with his grandparents.

Not saying a word, Jack's father studied both of the boys for several long moments. Their body language indicated trouble, but he knew not to ask for details in front of Jack's mother. Jack's father soon found out from his father that during the boys' stay, the house cat disappeared, they ate nearly all the food in the house, and they burned down the old feed shack. Jack's father decided not to ask CD for an explanation because CD was from the city, and he suspected that CD knew all the lies to get out of whatever city folk would be confronted with. Jack's father knew that many city slickers were just that way.

The next evening, Jack's father took his son to the side and asked him how he enjoyed their stay at his grandparents' house. Jack quickly confessed that CD had picked up the cat by its tail and swung it around and around, laughing as the cat tried to scurry away dizzily. Jack then told his father that CD raided the icebox at night and ate all the leftovers.

When Jack's father asked him about the feed shack, Jack said nothing as he picked at his fingernails. However, after his father promised not to spank him, he told him what had happened: "We were just playing, honestly, Poppa. CD found some candles and matches from the cupboard next to the stove. We took them out the old shack and lined up all the candles. Even though they were tall, I easily jumped over them, even when we lit them. But CD couldn't do it without knocking them over," Jack said with a little pride in his voice, but Jack's father face remained stern.

Jack continued, "And I got quicker each time, too. So CD started saying in a silly voice, 'Jack be nibble. Jack be quick. Jack jump over the candle stick.' I was having so much fun. CD tried hard, but he's so big, he couldn't jump high enough to clear the flames. When he knocked a candle down, we always blew it out," Jack paused. His father waited.

"But one set the straw on fire. We didn't have any water, and the fire spread quickly. So CD said that we'd better go down to the pond to get some water. When we came back, Grandfather was putting out the fire. He didn't look happy."

Jack's father almost sent CD home when he learned these details, but Jack's mother reminded him, "Boys will be boys." Knowing they had barely escaped serious trouble, CD and Jack played quietly near the house for a few days.

However, they soon fell back into their old routine, roaming the farm and playing just as they had done before.

On the last Saturday night of CD's stay, Jack's parents took the boys to a square dance at a local hall. Both CD and Jack loved the excitement. There were all kinds of food and colorful drinks. They were thrilled by the music and by seeing Jack's father play the fiddle with the band.

The next day, the boys spent the afternoon on the porch playing imaginary instruments. Then Jack asked for one of his mother's old wooden spoons. He loved the sound that he made hitting it against a solid piece of wood. CD found a branch and sang while he played his pretend guitar.

After three days of CD's singing, Jack said CD could scare the devil if he could hear him. CD kept on singing as he picked up another shorter stick, and as he pulled one stick along the other, he claimed he was the best fiddler in the world. Jack's mother soon told them that they would either have to get out of earshot or quit playing their instruments.

After lunch, both CD and Jack disappeared. Jack's mother was so pleased to have peace again that she did not ask them where they were going. While she enjoyed the quiet bustle of the farm, she did not notice that CD had slipped back into the house to grab Jack's father's fiddle.   Jack followed CD into the big, red barn, where Molly, the family's milk cow, hid from the afternoon sun in the corner of her stall, taking a nap. Although Jack did not really like how CD had teased Molly from the first day that he had arrived, Jack usually joined in, doing what most any boy would do to a cow: they took turns sneaking up behind her and then quickly running away after pulling her tail hard. Because of this, Molly watched for CD, and when she saw him nearing the barn, she quickly escaped to the shade of the woods nearby.

Smiling broadly, CD sat on a crate in the stall, placed the fiddle underneath his chin, and ran the bow across the strings. He pulled down and up steadily, making a strange, rhythmic screech. Jack started to pound in time on the side of the barn.

The house cat, May Bell, was stretched out near Molly's napping spot. Being very old, May Bell could barely hear the loud noise the two boys were making. From the reaction of her swinging tail, May Bell seemed pleased by what she could hear. They spent hours like this, happy to be making their so-called music.

On CD's last night on the farm, Jack's mother excused them after dinner to play one last time together. Daylight was fading, but they played under the big, bright harvest moon. While she cleaned up dinner, humming to herself, Jack's father reclined in his favorite chair and napped.

But quietly, CD snuck into the house and grabbed the fiddle and bow. Jack and CD ran out to the barn and jumped the gate to Molly's stall. They started to play their music again, softly at first, but they were soon screeching and banging loudly. Molly was trapped in the far corner of the stall, and unlike

May Bell, she could hear well. As soon as the noise began, she got up and started to move around the stall, looking an opening. As the intensity and volume grew, Molly paced more quickly.

In the glow of the huge, yellow moon, Molly looked for a gap between the two boys. At that moment, CD pulled the bow hard along the strings of the fiddle, making the loudest high-pitch sound anyone has ever heard. With that, Molly suddenly bolted between them, jumped over the fence, and ran into the woods.

Jack came running around the corner of the barn in the bright moonlight, crying out, "Poppa, Molly just jumped over the moon!"

CD returned to the city early the following morning, but Jack and his father spent days trying to coax Molly out of the woods and back to her stall. After she was satisfied that CD was not hiding in the corner with a fiddle, she went back to her familiar corner. However, she would not let anyone even so much as touch her for several more days. It was another two weeks before Jack's father could get any milk from her.

That fall, when Jack went to kindergarten, he told everyone how his cow had jump over the moon. He told the same story to anyone who would listen. Over the years, this story changed by word of mouth into the saying, "The cow jumped over the moon." The only thing left out was the name of the cow: Molly.

Interestingly, long after CD's exploits were forgotten, Molly still bolted at any loud noise. In fact, she jumped the stall's fence nearly other month. Jack's father finally sold Molly to a traveling Medicine Man, who returned to the farm years later and told Jack, "Molly jumped a six-foot fence late one evening. We looked for weeks, but we could not find her."

There are always different ways at looking at events around us.

The Legend of the Great Yellow Pumpkin

"Once a long time ago in New England, there was a young boy name Jack. This was the time before cars and planes, and people used only their feet and horses to go places. Now, Jack was only ten when the Great Yellow Pumpkin came to him."

Ling Chang stopped and looked at the large pumpkin to the left of him before he spoke again.

"Jack was a very bright boy and a good size for his age. He was a good boy, but he had one fault: he loved to daydream about the stories his father and grandfather would tell him by the fire at night before he would go to sleep. Jack loved to hear about goblins and strange goings-on in the forest at nighttime. Jack especially loved the tale about Little Red Riding Hood because of the Big Bad Wolf. Jack's red hair would nearly stand on end when his grandfather described the big, bulging eyes of the wolf and the large mouth with the razor sharp teeth, ready to get the poor little Red Riding Hood just before the lumberjack delivered his final judgment with his ax.

"Jack also loved stories about trolls underneath bridges and the so-called Boogiemen who dwell in the forest, the ones always looking for bad children.

"One fall day, it was October the 31st to be exact, Jack and his mother needed some salt and bacon from Jack's grandfather. Since his grandfather lived only a stone's throw away from Jack's place, he was usually given the task of running over to pick up whatever was needed," Ling Chang said, looking closely at Pat, who seemed to be trying to figure something out.

"Pat, a stone's throw can be just a couple of feet or even a couple of miles. The distance between Jack's folk's house and where he was going was about a mile or so. Jack could make the journey in no time, if he really tried, but he would always stop at the pond while going and coming back." Ling Chang paused, and Pat nodded.

Ling Chang continued, "Jack really enjoyed doing this task for several reasons. First of all, it gave him the opportunity to stop by the pond on the way and sit and daydream about the pirates his grandfather had told him many stories about. I think Jack wanted to be a pirate just like you wanted to be a cowboy when you were growing up.

"The other reason Jack liked this chore was because it gave him a sense of contributing to the household. He liked it when he could do something for a grown up, especially for his mother. You like that, too, right?" Pat nodded again.

"His mother Jane gave him the old cloth gunny sack to carry the salt, bacon, and whatever extra his grandmother might let them have. She always gave Jack something for doing this task for his mother. Leaving the house, Jack picked up the gunny sack, which was sitting by the door. Before shutting the door behind him, he checked his pocket for the knife he had gotten for his ninth birthday. His grandfather had shown him how to sharpen its edge so it would cut at the touch of its edge. With this knife, he had help to skin many a deer that his father and grandfather had killed. His mother often questioned why a boy needed to carry such a thing with him. Jack's reply was always the same: 'I might meet that Big Bad Wolf in the woods one day.' She would always smile at this answer. Even as he left his house this time, his mother did not fail to ask this question again, and she received the usual response. She did not know how important this knife would be to Jack this day on his trip back through the woods.

"While at his grandparent's house, his grandmother fed Jack some hot apple pie that she had just baked. She also gave Jack several small candles to help read his books. As he ate the pie, he listened closely as his grandfather told him about the big black bear that the townspeople were talking about tearing up the hot houses where they cured meat for the winter. He compared the big black bear to the Big Bad Wolf. Jack's eyes grew bigger as his grandfather described the Big Bad Wolf again—in detail.

"Before leaving, Jack's grandfather gave him a pumpkin to carry. His mother wanted to make pumpkin pie for the family. Jack left in plenty of time to get home before dark. True to form, he stopped by the pond. Jack placed the gunny sack by the tree next to his favorite spot. He did not think of pirates but of fighting the big black bear. After taking care of the bear, he would battle the Big Bad Wolf, either finishing him off with his sharp knife or making him run away to return and fight Jack another day.

"Darkness fell early in New England, but Jack did not notice. He was only concerned with fighting the big black bear or the Big Bad Wolf. After Jack fought off the bear and the wolf several times, he finally noticed it was getting dark, and the cool fall night wind had started to blow. He wondered if he could make it home by dark. Jack did not like the dark because this was when the Big Bad Wolf could easily sneak up on him or something else could stalk him without his seeing it.

"He started down the path to his house. Even in the twilight, he could see the track that he had worn over the past several years. The sky was growing darker by the second. Jack stopped, looked up, and saw a full moon. This, he thought, was when the Big Bad Wolf really liked to roam the woods. His grandfather had told him so many times.

"Jack looked around again. Now he could barely see the shrubs and trees on the side of the path. What was he to do? If he could not see the path that he was traveling, then he would be lost in the woods until the sun came up. By then, the Big Bad Wolf might have finished him off," Ling Chang said, smiling at Pat's wide eyes.

"Jack's heart started to beat faster. His mother would be wondering if the Indians had met a couple of weeks ago had gotten him, and her little Jack O'Leary would be no more. His father would be worried that a poison snake had bitten him or that the cougar that they had seen a month ago had gotten him.

"Jack started to walk quickly. Then he felt something grab at his left arm. The first thing that entered his mind was that the Big Bad Wolf was trying to seize him. Jack yanked his arm back and turned to run. His heart sank as he felt two large arms grabbing him. Jack thought the big black bear must have grabbed him with both of his big arms. Jack almost dropped the gunny sack and the pumpkin he was carrying.

"His heart rose a little when he realized neither the Big Bad Wolf nor the big black had attacked him. He had only walked into a large, spindly shrub. After Jack untangled himself, he took a deep breath and stood motionless for several minutes. He could hear his heart beating.

"Jack had to figure out what to do next. He suddenly remembered he had some candles and matches in the gunny sack. He lit a candle, but the cool night wind blew it out straight away. He tried this several times, and each time the wind blew it out.

"Jack stood motionless. He had to figure out how to protect the flame of the candle against the wind. Suddenly, he remembered how his mother cut open pumpkins. It was hollow! He could put the candle in there so that the wind would not blow it out again.

"He took his knife out of his pocket and sliced a large hole in the top of the pumpkin. He turned the pumpkin over, shaking out nearly all of the seeds. He lit the candle and placed it inside. The flame flickered for a moment, but it died out. He lit it again, and the same thing happened.

"As the darkness closed in on him a little more, Jack remembered his grandfather working on a

kerosene lantern and telling him fire needs air to burn.
So Jack swiftly cut two holes on one side of the
pumpkin, big enough to let light out, but not enough to
let the wind in. He tried to light the candle again. It
still did not burn long. Jack made one more cut, just
in between and down from the two other cuts. The
same thing happened; the candle went out.

"Jack's heart was beating faster. The big black
bear or the Big Bad Wolf was probably waiting for him
in the dark. He ran his blade under the three holes,
making two long cuts that joined at each end. He lit
the candle again. Now, the flame was tall and bright."

Pat smiled at Jack's victory.

"But when Jack lifted the pumpkin up quickly,
the candle went out yet again. His heart sank into his
chest yet again. He was finished, and the Big Bad
Wolf would have him for his dinner if the big black
bear did not get him first.

"Jack's hands shook as lit the candle one more
time, but this time, he placed the top that he had cut
out back where had cut it out. The candle did not go
out. He was safe, and he could find his way home.
He secured the gunny sack to his belt. He held the
pumpkin up with both hands and looked for the path
he had walk so many times.

"Jack walked slowly at first. He was afraid that
the candle would go out. He heard terrifying noises
all around him. He looked quickly every few seconds
to his left and to his right. Jack knew that the big
black bear and the Big Bad Wolf would be afraid of
the light and the fire that could be seen through the
opening of the pumpkin.

"'What a Great Yellow Pumpkin!" Jack chuckled
to himself. 'The Great Yellow Pumpkin has given me
a light to see my way back home. It has scared way
the big black bear and the Big Bad Wolf.'

55

"Jack's arms started to hurt from holding up the Great Yellow Pumpkin when he saw the lights of the burning fire at his home. His mother was on the front porch, calling out for him. When she saw the light from Jack's candle through the woods by the house, she raced down the steps. She hugged and kissed him and told him that he could not go to his grandparent's house in the afternoon anymore.

"Jack was in luck that his father was out looking for him, but by the time he returned home, Jack was asleep, his lantern flickering beside him."

Pat relaxed at the news, and Ling Chang smiled.

"The next day at school, Jack told his schoolmates about his great adventure from the night before. Yes, he told them about the Great Yellow Pumpkin that he had created and how he had scared off the big black bear that was tearing up the farmers' property. He also told about how the Big Bad Wolf had tried to grab his arm once, but the Big Bad Wolf had run away when Jack had pulled out his sharp knife. Soon, everyone at school knew all about Jack's adventure.

"Over the following weeks and years, the legend of the Great Yellow Pumpkin grew. Jack showed other boys how to make a Great Yellow Pumpkin. The power of the Great Yellow Pumpkin grew and grew to the point that it could protect little boys and girls from the darkness and from any evil that would try to harm them."

We have a special something inside us that will help us figure out any problem.

Chance the Bear

When the brightest star ever shone in the northern sky, once upon a time and long ago, all the animals in the forest could sense an excitement in the air.

The lions were roaming the grassy plains roaring, telling of an exciting event that had taken place. The birds in the forest were flying from branch to branch, singing at the top of their voices. The monkeys were chattering throughout the trees, jumping from tree to tree. The rhinoceros were jumping into the nearby streams and splashing water on to the shore. The elephants were at the same watering hole, drinking their trunks full of water and spraying the rhinoceroses and any other animals that came in range.

In the forest beyond the plains, there was a small bear that was only a year old. He listened to all of the other bears' roaring, telling others in the distance about this great happening.

Chance only measured three feet tall when he stood up on his hind legs. Being so young and small, he did not fully understand the greatness of the happening that had taken place and the reason for the bright star in the northern sky.

Between the roars of his extended family, Chance learned from Mama Bear that his parents would be going to see what everyone was so excited about. Father Bear told him to stay in the den, and they would be back in a short while.

However, Chance was like any youngster—curiosity soon got the best of him.

Mama Bear had tried to teach him at a very early age that this curiosity would always get him into trouble. (This began after he had gotten his head caught in an old hollow log while looking for honey.) Yet Chance still had not learned his lesson about his curiosity. When his mother had gathered up some of the best and sweetest honey to be given as a present, he knew he had to see this happening. Chance heard Mama Bear tell Papa Bear that she wanted them to show their best and to give their best so they would honor this blessed event.

Mama Bear said she had heard that the birds were going to sing for the boy child, and the lions were going to protect him. Chance listened carefully as Mama Bear listed what all the other animals were going to do to show their appreciation of this great event.

As soon as Mama Bear and Papa Bear left the den, Chance's curiosity overcame him—as it usually does in a small bear. Chance thought that if this is the greatest event of all time, he did not want to be left out.

So Chance looked around the den, wondering what he could bring to this affair. He did not have anything really, nothing that was his, nothing special. He had a few toys that had been his brother's, but they were all worn out or broken. Finally, he eyes settled on the toy drum that Papa Bear had given him as soon as he could stand upright and hold the toy drum by himself.

Chance grabbed the toy drum and his drum sticks. He eased his nose out of the den, sniffing for trouble—or worse, his mother coming back to check on him. Sensing nothing of concern, he trotted out and followed his parents at what he felt was a safe distance. However, his parents soon discovered that they had a travelling companion after they heard Chance's crying because he had wedged his head into another hollow log that smelled a lot like honey.

After Mama Bear scolded him about his curiosity, Papa Bear decided not to send him back to the den. They agreed that if Chance was so keen to see the great event, then he should come along. However, they warned him that the journey would be a long one.

After walking for many days, they arrived at last at the great event. Chance was surprised. With all the excitement and the ways that everyone wanted to give their best, Chance expected to see a very fancy place. He was disappointed to find only a rundown stable with some sheep, cows, and a donkey in it. In the middle of the stable, a man and a woman sat on either side of a makeshift cradle lined with straw.

Soon after the Bear family arrived, they watched quietly as three men with crowns leave, riding past on the backs of camels. Chance overheard one of the men claim that he was certain this was the one that they had been waiting for. The other men nodded their heads.

Chance saw the lions lying on the nearby hillside and the birds perching in different places in and on the stable. They were all silent now. Mama Bear went into the stable to place the honey on a bench near the cradle. The gift sat with all kinds of nuts and fruits that many of the animals had brought to honor this event.

Chance noticed that the woman was picking something up from the cradle. A strange light fell, showing the baby. The baby started to cry, and the woman looked concerned. The man looked at her and at the animals in the stable.

The lions got up and started their slow pacing. They each made a low rumbling noise so as not to frighten the small one even more, but he continued to cry. The birds began a chorus of soft whistles, hoping to soothe the child, but the child's cry grew louder. The woman gave him some of the honey that Chance's mother had brought, but he cried louder still.

Suddenly, the sound of a soft drum roll tapped against the baby's cries. As the drum's volume increased, the baby's cries decreased. All the animals turned to look where the drumming sound was coming from. Chance was standing in the entrance to the stable, playing his drum.

Soon the baby's whimpers faded. The woman smiled at Chance, while he continued to play his gentle rhythm on his toy drum. She laid the baby back in the cradle, and he went to sleep.

Papa Bear and Mama Bear proudly led Chance back to their den. She kept telling him that this was one time that Chance's curiosity had turned out for the good. All of the other animals left that place, too, returning to their dens, nests. and trees.

To this day, all of the animals tell the story of Chance the Drummer Bear who played for the Christ Child.

Each of us has a special gift to offer others.

The Magical Pebbles

One spring day, the Great Wise man, An Ho, came to the village where I was living. He just appeared one day.

He first appeared to an old woman who had just lost her husband of thirty years. She was picking at the weeds in her garden when he asked her, "Why are you sad, woman?" Of course, she told him how she missed her husband. She said she would look for him to come to the house after he had worked the fields and hoped he would hold her in the evening.

An Ho did not say a word to the woman after she had explained her deep sorrow. He just turned and walked away. The woman was totally surprised at this strange man. She did not understand why he had not said anything to comfort her in her sorrow.

The next person An Ho approached was a merchant who was yelling at the top of his lungs with no one around. He bellowed about how the ruling elders had increased the tax on the merchandise he sold to his customers.

"Why are you so upset and not at peace?" An Ho asked the merchant. The merchant told him about the elders' new tax. He grumbled about how they seemed to create a new tax every year. He went on to complain out trying to put money away for his retirement. With every word, the merchants' voice grew louder and louder.

An Ho just stood silent and listen to this man yell and scream about his dilemma. The merchant had heard about An Ho, the wise man who roamed the countryside, so he was surprised by the silent reaction. Certainly, the wise man would say something to solve the problem he had. But An Ho just listened and, again, left without saying a word. This left the merchant even more frustrated and angry with the situation that he was.

An Ho then walked down the street and met a young man who was putting together some kind of machinery that had many parts. The expression on the man's face revealed what he was experiencing. His eyes were roving from piece to piece, examining the shapes and size, trying to determine what to do with the assortment of parts in his hands. Looking up from the pieces, the young man was the first to speak: "Well, are you just going to stand there? I have spent all morning trying to put this piece and that piece together, and nothing seems to fit to make complete working whatever-it-is." The young man held up his hands, perhaps expecting An Ho to study them; however, the wise man merely stood and listened.

"My patience is almost gone! My boss demands that I put this machinery together, or else I will lose my job. He says it is as simple as falling off a log, but I do not think it is so. Are you just going to stand there?!" the young man snapped.

Once again, An Ho remained silent during the tirade. He then turned slowly and left the young man still holding several parts in each hand. The young man threw the pieces in his hand on the ground.

An HO came next to a sad young woman, sitting in a bamboo chair. She was looking down the path that left and entered the village. He asked, "Why are you crying, my fair lady?"

"My young husband has gone to war," she replied tearfully. "I don't know if he will return. I miss his touch and his love for me. I feel so empty inside."

An Ho smiled and touched the young woman on her head with his open hand and turn and left without saying a word. He then left the village and did not return for several days.

During this time, An Ho went down to a small stream nearby. He waded in, and from the stream bed, he retrieved four smooth stones. Next to his fire at his encampment, he patiently worked his knife on the stones, patiently etching a different word on each.

He returned to the village one evening just before dusk. He found the home of the old woman who had lost her husband of many years. He knocked on her thatched door, and the old woman opened it, wearing her house clothes and an apron. She did not say anything, for An Ho spoke first: "I came the other day. You spoke of your loss. I have come to give this comfort."

An Ho held both hands open in front of him so that the woman could see that nothing was there or hidden. Suddenly, he closed both hands in a fist, which he dipped into one pouch of the old woman's apron. He withdrew his hands, and then one of the pebbles had appeared in the wise man's palms. The woman could see the word "comfort" inscribed on it.

An Ho handed the pebble to the old woman. He said nothing else to her. He bowed first his head and then the upper half of his body. He turned and ambled away. Tears fell from the woman's eyes; someone had understood her sorrow and had given her comfort, a comfort that she could cherish the rest of her life.

An Ho went next to find the merchant who had been yelling. As An Ho approached, the merchant did not speak. An Ho spoke first: "I have come back. I know that you are worried that I could not solve our dilemma about the new taxes the elders have put on you. I have come to give you what you wanted."

"Have you money that I can pay the elders or give my customers?" the merchant asked hopefully.

"No, but I have something better, and you have it inside yourself," An Ho replied. He spread his arms wide and upward above his shoulders so that the merchant could see his empty hands. He quickly balled each into a tight fist and moved toward the merchant.

"It is in your money pouch on your left side," An Ho announced as he reached into merchant's money pouch. "Ah, here it is!"

An Ho opened his left, exposing a small pebble with the word "peace" etched into it. "You have it always in you," An Ho reminded the merchant. "You only have to let it grow. There are few things in this world you can control—one of them is you."

A stunned expression worked on the merchant's face. An Ho dropped his head in silence and then bowed half way with his upper body. As quickly as he came, he left, leaving the merchant there still and speechless.

An Ho went then to the young man who had been putting together the pieces of machinery. Seeing the wise man walking toward him, the young man called out, "I see you're back now after I've nearly figured this out."

An Ho smiled and said, "I see you have accomplished much since I was last here. I have something for you that you will to need to finish this job. It will also help you with the other tasks you will undertake during your life."

An Ho lifted up both his arms with his hands wide open where the young man could see that his hands were empty. An Ho buried his hands deep into the young man's tool box. He withdrew his hands, each in a tight fist, and said, "You have had this all the time, yet you have not used it in your work."

An Ho opened his left hand where a pebble sat —on it, "patience."

"If you use this, which you already have, you will accomplish all your tasks quickly and with ease," An Ho said as he gave the pebble to the young man. The young man stared at the pebble as An Ho bowed his head and then upper body.

An Ho slipped away in silence while the young man studied the pebble.

Finally, An Ho found the young woman still sitting at the edge of the village, waiting for her love to come back from war.

"You are where I thought you would be," An Ho said in a quiet, tender voice. The young woman said nothing to An Ho. She simply stared at the empty road.

"I have something for you," An Ho said. "After I left this village, I went to meditate on what I had experience here. I came to give what certain people were looking for in life. I have come to you last, for you search for the greatest of all the gifts in this world." As An Ho spoke, he lifted up both arms, revealing the emptiness of his large hands. He closed them and placed them gently behind each of the young woman's ears.

"But you have the greatest of gifts," An Ho said, pulling his arms back slowly as he opened his hands. The last of the pebbled rested in his palm, the word "love" cut into it.

"Take this," An Ho told the young woman. She did, and looked at it.

"You are complete with your love," An Ho said. "No distance can put a wedge between your two loves. Until he returns, go and share this love with the people in this village."

Again, he bowed his head and then half of his body toward the young woman.

An Ho turned and walked down the path that led out of the village. The young woman rose up from the chair and watched the wise man slowly disappear down the path.

Clasping her pebble, she went throughout the village, telling everyone about the wise man and what he had told her.

Each of us has the answer with us.